DIVING
is for me

DIVING is for me

Carole S. Briggs

photographs by
Greg Sutter

Lerner Publications Company Minneapolis

The author wishes to thank Kent Oldenburg, diving coach, and Denny Hanson, pool manager, Ridgewood pool; Stephanie Leonard; and J.V. McKenna.

To Eileen Melnikov

LIBRARY OF CONGRESS CATALOGING IN PUBLICATION DATA

Briggs, Carole S.
Diving is for me.

(A Sports for me book)
Summary: J.V. and Stephanie discuss their experiences learning to dive at their local pool.
1. Diving—Juvenile literature. [1. Diving]
I. Sutter, Greg, ill. II. Title. III. Series: Sports for me books.
GV838.6.B74 1983 797.2′3 82-17242
ISBN 0-8225-1135-5 (lib. bdg.)

Manufactured in the United States of America

International Standard Book Number: 0-8225-1135-5
Library of Congress Catalog Card Number: 82-17242

2 3 4 5 6 7 8 9 10 91 90 89 88 87 86 85 84

Hello! I'm J.V., and this is my friend Stephanie. Last summer we took a diving class together. I'd like to tell you about the diving skills we learned.

Divers dive into a pool from a **spring-board.** The springboard that beginners usually use is 1 meter (39 inches) above the water. It is called a springboard because it springs, or bounces, up and down.

Most springboards have a wheel underneath that moves a round metal tube called a **fulcrum.** The position of the fulcrum controls how much bounce the board will have.

If you turn the wheel to move the fulcrum further back, the board will have more bounce. If you move the fulcrum toward the end of the board that is nearest to the water, the board will have less bounce. Most children need bouncy springboards. Our bodies are light, and we can't push down on the board as hard as adults can.

The **high board** is a springboard for more experienced divers. The high board is 3 meters (about 10 feet) above the water. Beginners shouldn't climb the high board until they've learned several dives. And there should always be an experienced swimmer or diver watching when anyone climbs the high board.

Many swimming pools have a special area for diving called a **diving well.** Diving wells are usually 10 to 14 feet deep. Jets of water come out from the sides of the well to make ripples on the surface of the water. The ripples help the diver to see the surface of the water more clearly instead of just the bottom of the pool. This helps divers to judge the distance of their dives.

Our diving instructor's name was Kent. Kent was an excellent diver who also taught diving to beginners. A diving instructor like Kent is often called a **coach**.

The first thing Kent told us was that diving should be done *only* in deep water. We must dive in the diving well or in the deep end of a regular pool. If we dove into shallow water, we could get hurt quite badly.

Kent explained that we should always check the depth of the water before diving. Extend your arm up over your head and measure the distance from your feet to your fingertips. Never dive into water that is less than 2 feet deeper than that measurement.

Kent also said that we should never try a dive before he taught us how it is done. There should always be a lifeguard or an experienced diver around to watch us practice, too.

Being able to swim well is a must for all divers. So before starting lessons, Kent tested our swimming skills. First we had to **tread water.** Treading water is a way of keeping your head above water with your body in an upright position. The arms are moved in figure eights near the top of the water, and a scissors kick is done with the legs.

Next we had to swim two lengths of the pool. We all passed that test, so we were officially admitted to the diving class. Were we happy!

Kent said that the body is one's most important piece of diving equipment. To keep our bodies from getting sore from all the work that diving takes, Kent had us do **land conditioning** exercises. These exercises help prevent strains and pulls.

First Kent showed us an exercise to help strengthen our ankles and feet. We crouched on the ground and balanced on our toes. Our hands were placed flat on the ground, and then we pushed up with them.

Toe touching and touching the head to the knees help stretch the backs of the legs. These exercises also make it easier to bend at the waist during a dive.

We warmed up our hip muscles by pressing each knee over the opposite leg. We did this until we felt a nice stretch, but we didn't force anything.

A diver's stomach muscles need to be strong, too, so Kent had us do **V-sits.** We sat on the ground and brought our arms and legs together in a *V.* This was hard. We were really getting a workout!

The last exercise Kent showed us was easier. We put our hands flat against a fence. Then we put one leg back and pushed that heel up and down several times. This stretched the big muscle in the lower leg to help prevent cramps when toes are pointed in a dive.

The next time we met, Kent taught us the beginning steps of diving. He explained that every dive must begin with the right **stance.** The stance is the way you stand on the board before you dive. A good stance for any dive is to stand straight with the head up, the chin level, and the eyes looking at the end of the board.

Next come the **approach** and **hurdle.** These are the moves taken as you get ready to spring off the board. Kent told us that all forward dives begin with the same approach and hurdle. Start by taking the proper stance. Look at the end of the board and take three walking steps toward it. This is the **approach.**

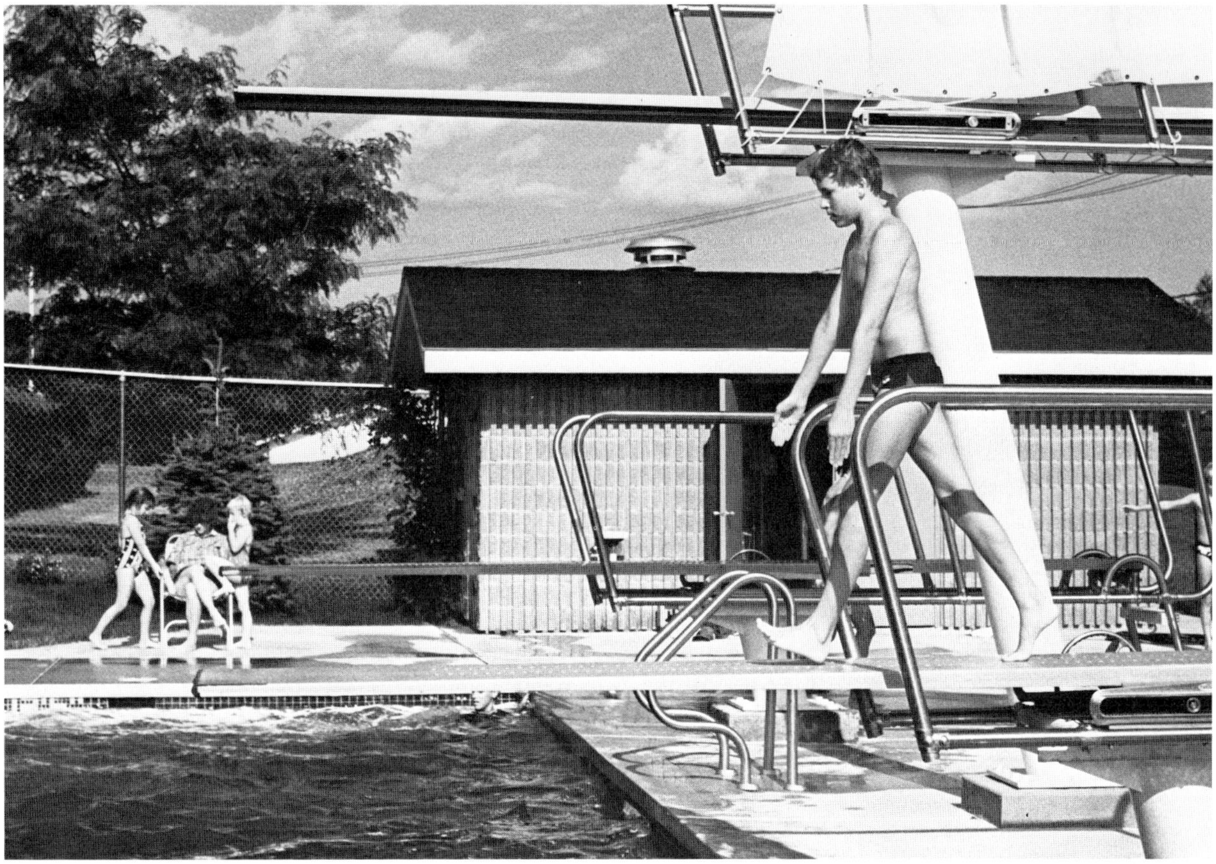

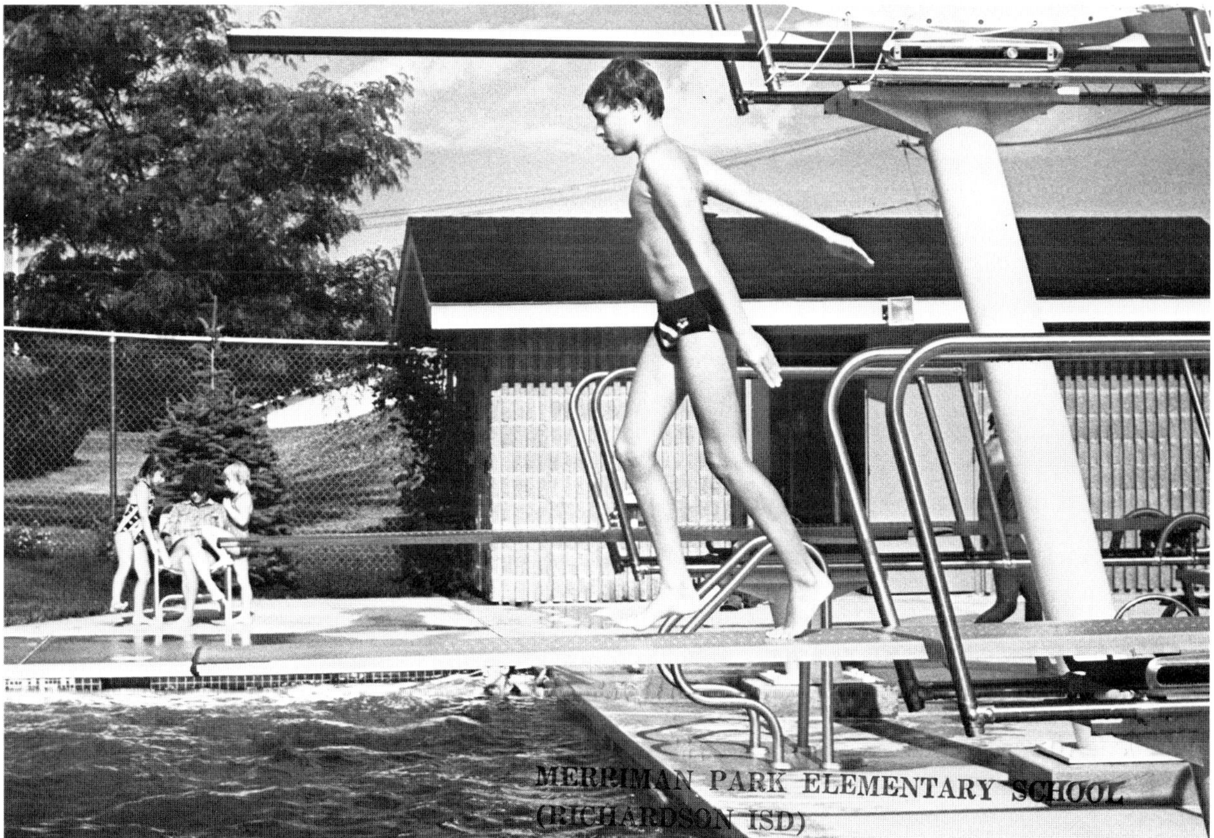

As you take the third step, swing your arms up, bring one knee up, and jump with the other leg. This is the **hurdle**. To get the most **lift**, jump as close to the end of the board as you can. Lift is how high the springy board helps carry you into the air.

At the highest point of the hurdle, the toes are pointed, the legs are straight, and the arms are in a *V* above the head. Bounce back down on the board with both feet, and bring your arms just behind you. Then swing your arms forward and push hard up and off the board.

Next we learned the **takeoff.** The takeoff occurs as the diver's body first leaves the board. It comes right after the hurdle. For a good takeoff, press down on the board with your legs, bring the chest up, and let the board lift you into the air.

As you go up, arms are in a *T* position and toes are pointed. Next thing you know, you're off the board and on your way to the water! We practiced by entering the water feet first with our arms at our sides. We would learn our first real dive at our next lesson.

Finally the day for our lesson came. We watched carefully as Kent showed us how to do a **forward dive, layout position.**

Layout position means that at the highest point of the dive, your body is stretched straight and level with the water. Your body isn't bent anywhere, and your arms are straight out. We began the forward dive with the steps we had already learned.

Kent next explained that the takeoff controls the **line of flight.** Line of flight is the path that the body travels through the air. As you spring upward during takeoff for a forward dive, look up, point your toes, and keep your arms in a *T* position. Then bring your arms over your head and point them towards the water.

The way your body goes into the water is called the **entry.** A good entry includes straight legs, pointed toes, and arms together over the ears. Arms should reach towards the bottom of the pool.

When it was my friend Katie's turn to try the forward dive, layout position, she landed on her stomach. Does that sting! When we knew she wasn't hurt badly, everyone teased her by yelling "Belly flop!" Belly flops happen when you don't keep your head down as you reach the water. Nearly all beginning divers do belly flops now and then.

We practiced the forward dive over and over. Each time we tried it, Kent had us work on different parts of the dive so that we'd get used to doing all the steps.

Kent told us that there are three body positions for dives. We had already done the front dive in layout position. The other diving positions we would learn are the **pike position** and the **tuck position.**

The **forward dive, pike position,** is sometimes called the **jackknife.** You use the same stance, approach, and hurdle used with other forward dives. As your body moves upward off the board, bend at the hips right away. Bring your arms toward your legs to form a triangle with your body.

As you start to come toward the water, open the pike by kicking up your legs and pointing your toes at the sky. Your arms should be together over the head and ears. As you enter the water, reach for the bottom of the pool.

We all practiced hard between lessons. Kent thought we were doing well. We were excited when he told us we were ready to learn the **back dive, layout position.**

First we learned a special stance for all back dives. Kent had us stand backwards on the end of the board, rising on our toes with our arms at shoulder level.

To do the back dive, swing your arms down and behind you. Bend your knees, keep your elbows straight, and lift your arms fast. At the same time, push your legs hard against the board.

Kent explained that on takeoff it is important to press down hard with the legs. Shooting your arms straight overhead helps give your takeoff added height.

Then, as you arch backward into the air, move your arms to a *T* position. The head should tilt back at the top of the line of flight. The legs will begin to lift. As you come down, bring the arms together overhead and point your toes. You will enter the water at a slight angle. The body is stretched headfirst toward the bottom of the pool, and arms are together over the ears.

The back dive is a hard dive. It is not a natural feeling to go from standing to being upside down and backwards. So many people try to twist their heads or upper bodies forward to see the water. Doing this may make the dive *seem* less frightening, but you won't be doing it correctly. It is important to practice each step of the dive many times until you get it right.

We were getting more used to the feeling of diving backwards. So Kent taught us the **back somersault, tuck position.** This is a complicated dive, so we listened carefully as Kent explained it.

For the backward tuck somersault, you need a good hard push with the legs to send the body upward. Then you go into the tuck position.

In the tuck position, your knees are against your chest, and your arms grasp the lower front of your legs. When you are rolled into a ball, you must arch your head toward the water. Kent explained that the spinning motion is caused by **momentum.** Momentum means that once you start moving in a certain way, the weight of your body causes that movement to continue.

As you push off the springboard and arch your head backwards, your body will spin in that direction. When you begin to face the water, kick your legs straight out. Enter the water feet first with your arms at your sides and your toes pointed. I loved practicing this dive. It felt neat to be spinning backwards through the air.

Later on in the summer Kent taught us the **inward dive, pike position.** It's called *inward* because you do the pike movement facing the board. It is important to lift well away from the board for this dive. That's hard, though, because there's no hurdle to help you.

Kent stressed the importance of pushing hard with the legs in order to get plenty of height for good body position. As the hips rise, the arms come down and touch the toes. This forms the pike. The arms then circle out to the sides. As they come back together, the legs are lifted above the head. The body should be completely straight during the entry.

The last dives we learned were called **twist dives.** For these dives, we had to think hard about what we were doing. There is a lot to do in the short time you spend sailing through the air!

First we learned the **forward dive, layout, with half twist.** A **twist** is a full vertical turn of the body. You leave the board facing forward, twist in midair, and enter as you did for the back dive. The stance, approach, and hurdle for twists are the same as for the other forward dives.

The twisting motion is begun at the moment of takeoff. As you leave the board, your arms should be in a *T.* Use your muscles to twist your upper body, and tilt to one side like a turning airplane. Twist one shoulder back quite hard and look down along the forward arm.

As you start to drop from the top of the line of flight, continue turning your body to make a complete half turn. Arch your back, tilt your head back, and look at the water. Then put your arms together and stretch for an entry as if you were doing a back dive.

One day, Kent showed us a dive that we might get to learn when we're older. It's a hard dive, and Kent did it from the high board. This dive was the **forward one-and-a-half somersault, pike position.**

Kent began the dive by using the stance, approach, and hurdle for the forward dives, but he arched his arms slightly forward. On takeoff, his body went into the pike position with arms grasping the legs. He let the momentum of the hurdle carry him around one and a half times. He stayed in pike position, with the hands grasping the legs, the whole time he was spinning.

As he faced the water for the second time, he opened the pike. He lifted his legs toward the sky and entered the water head first. His hands reached for the bottom of the pool, and his toes were pointed.

The dive was very exciting! We all look forward to learning it ourselves someday. It takes a lot of practice to become a good diver. But *never* practice without a diver or lifeguard watching.

Every summer there's a swimming and diving **meet**, or contest, at the pool where we have lessons. Swimmers and divers from other pools in the city come to compete with us. In the diving competition, points are given for each dive. The highest possible score is 10. That score is very hard to get.

Divers are given points for each part of their dive—the stance, approach, hurdle, takeoff, flight, and entry. These points are multiplied by the **degree of difficulty,** or how hard the dive is. This gives a final score for the dive. For example, the forward dive in pike position is worth 1.2 times your score. A back dive in pike position is worth 1.6 times your score.

We entered the diving competition to test our skills. It was exciting to see our friends doing their very best diving. It was also fun to watch the older divers do more difficult dives. When the meet was over, we were tired but happy. Our team had done well. We think diving is an exciting sport, and we can hardly wait to learn more dives. Diving is for us!

Words about DIVING

APPROACH: The beginning steps for a forward dive

DEGREE OF DIFFICULTY: How hard a dive is

DIVING WELL: A special pool area, with deep water, used especially for diving

ENTRY: The part of a dive in which the body goes into the water

FULCRUM: A metal tube under a springboard that controls how much bounce the board will have

HIGH BOARD: A springboard that is 3 meters (about 10 feet) above the water

HURDLE: The upward movement after a hard jump on the end of a board

INWARD DIVES: Dives begun by standing on the end of the board with the back towards the water. The diver then enters the water facing away from the board.

LAND CONDITIONING: Exercises to strengthen the body for diving

LAYOUT POSITION: A dive position in which the body is held parallel to the water at the top of the line of flight

LIFT: The amount of height achieved during the hurdle

LINE OF FLIGHT: The path the diver travels from the board to the water

MEET: A diving contest

MOMENTUM: The force of a moving object

PIKE POSITION: A dive position in which the body is bent at the waist

SPRINGBOARD: A diving board that springs, or bounces, up and down

STANCE: The way of standing on the board before a dive

TAKEOFF: The action of leaving the board and going towards the water

TREADING WATER: A way of keeping the head above the water with the body in an upright position

TUCK POSITION: A dive position in which the knees are brought to the chest and the head is arched toward the water

ABOUT THE AUTHOR

CAROLE S. BRIGGS enjoys writing books for children. She is an avid SCUBA diver, and has done SCUBA diving in Tahiti and on Australia's Great Barrier Reef. A graduate of the University of Wisconsin, Ms. Briggs lives in Madison, Wisconsin, with her husband and two children.

ABOUT THE PHOTOGRAPHER

GREG SUTTER graduated from Layton School of Art and Design in Milwaukee, Wisconsin. He has worked in every phase of photography, including studio, commercial, journalistic, and artistic. His specialty is underwater photography. Mr. Sutter lives in Madison, Wisconsin.

Briggs, Carole S.

Diving is for me